supe

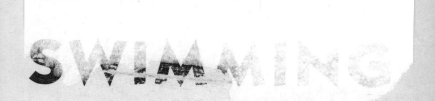

SWIMMING

Clive Gifford

Illustrations by Lorna Barnard
Cartoons by Ken O'Brien
Consultant: Garry Seghers
Swimming Teachers' Association

Hodder
Children's
Books

a division of Hodder Headline

Text copyright 1998 © Clive Gifford
Illustrations copyright 1998 © Lorna Barnard
Cartoon illustrations copyright 1998 © Ken O'Brien
This edition published by Hodder Children's Books 2000

Consultant: Garry Seghers, Development Co-ordinator, Swimming
Teachers' Association

Series design by Fiona Webb
Book design by Don Martin
Project editor: Lyn Coutts

The right of Clive Gifford, Lorna Barnard and Ken O'Brien to be identified
as the author and illustrators of the work has been asserted by them in
accordance with the Copyright, Designs and Patents Act 1988.

10 9 8 7 6 5 4 3 2 1

A catalogue record for this book is available from the British Library.

ISBN: 0 340 791616

Printed by Clays Ltd., St. Ives plc

Hodder Children's Books
a division of Hodder Headline Limited
338 Euston Road
London NW1 3BH

About the author

Clive was off sick the day confidence in the water was handed out. He struggled in school swimming lessons and was the world record holder for the biggest bellyflop ever when he first attempted to dive.

Feeling humiliated, Clive kept as dry as a roasted peanut until he was ten. Then while on holiday he suddenly discovered the joys of swimming. Bitten by the bug, Clive gained a number of distance swimming badges and joined lifesaving classes.

Now he has settled on doing what he loves best: swimming for fun. Swimming and surfing, swimming and canoeing, swimming and water volleyball and just plain swimming – when Clive takes the plunge it is for the best of reasons – to enjoy himself.

Clive loves swimming best in the sea. Japanese whaling ships have occasionally eyed-up his large, blubbery frame, but, so far, his surprisingly good stroke technique has kept him just out of harpoon range.

Introduction

Why swim?

Unlike most animals, humans have the amazing ability to enjoy being on land and in water. Being able to swim means you can take part in a whole range of cool activities like canoeing, surfing and sailing. You may even be able to help others who get into difficulty in the water.

Swimming is also one of the best ways to keep fit. It builds your heart and lungs and uses lots of different muscle groups without straining them like other exercising can. People with disabilities or who are recovering from accidents often use swimming as part of their therapy. Top cyclists and athletes use swimming in their regular training.

Best of all, swimming is brilliant fun. The millions of people around the world who regularly swim agree. You can swim by yourself or with friends. You can enter competitions, join a swim club and learn to snorkel or play water polo. And on holiday, there's nothing better than taking a dip! Whether you swim for gold or swim to cool off, fun is guaranteed!

Clive.

Contents

Get ready for fun!

So you want to be a swimmer, do you? Another Mark Spitz, perhaps? Spitz won seven swimming gold medals in the 1972 Olympics, an achievement unlikely ever to be equalled. Or perhaps you want to follow in the wake of Captain Matthew Webb. More than 100 years ago he succeeded in a feat of swimming daring by crossing the English Channel when the experts said it couldn't be done.

Then again, like me, you may want to swim just for fun, as a passport to healthy exercise and a host of water-based activities, even just lazing around in the hotel pool while on holiday.

Whatever you plan to do, there are some basics that every swimmer must know about. So, dig out your swimming kit, check out your pool, and let's get started.

What to wear?

A swimsuit is not absolutely
necessary but is a good idea in
public pools and on beaches!

For boys, choosing a swimsuit
is pretty simple. You'll need
swimming trunks for serious
swimming. Shorts create lots of
drag in the water and slow you
down. Super-long shorts can
even restrict your movement.

For girls, there's far more
choice. For serious swimming, avoid bikinis and skimpy
fashion swimsuits. Plump instead for a swimsuit with a high
neckline that makes you more streamlined in the water.

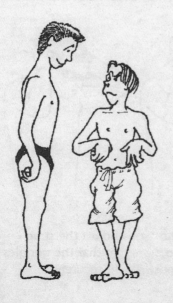

Most swimsuits are made
of stretchy materials like
cotton mixed with Lycra.
Make sure your swimsuit is
comfortable and fits well.
Buy your swimsuit from a
good sports or specialist
swimming shop, and with
care it will last for ages.

With your swimsuit, towel,
soap and shampoo you're
all set. Or are you? Here's
some other swim kit you
may like to splash out on.

LIFE'S A DRAG WITHOUT A CAP

Some pools insist on a swimcap if you have long hair. These are made of rubber and, when dry after your swim, need to be sprinkled with talcum powder – they will be easier to put on next time. Top swimmers use swimcaps to cut the tiny amount of extra drag their hair and ears create in the water.

A SIGHT FOR SORE EYES

Goggles help many swimmers who find it hard or painful to keep their eyes open under the water. Get a lightweight pair with a comfortable, adjustable strap. Most of all, make sure they fit and don't leak. Tinted pairs are handy if you swim mainly outside in strong sunlight.

Some people find spitting into the goggles then rinsing them stops them misting up as much. Always put your goggles on in the way shown below. When removing your goggles, put thumbs under the head strap at the side of head. Slide thumbs to the back of head and lift elastic from back to front of head.

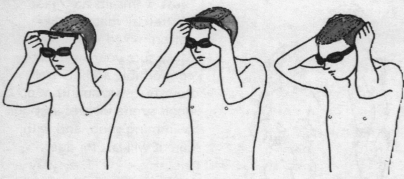

▲ STEP 1
Place the eyepieces of the goggles carefully over your eyes.

▲ STEP 2
Then stretch the strap over head using both hands.

▲ STEP 3
Adjust the strap so that the goggles fit securely.

PUT A PLUG IN IT

Ear plugs help prevent ear infections from pool water. Older types were made from hard plastic but now you can get soft ones which mould themselves to fit your ears.

Many people find a nose clip helps them to breath through their mouth better. It's up to you. They're not essential. Both nose clips and ear plugs are cheap so always buy your own and never use anyone else's. Buy a spare set and keep them safe.

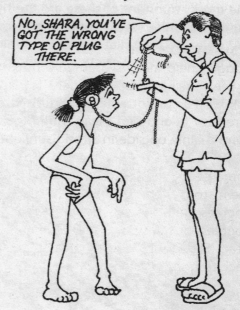

NO, SHARA, YOU'VE GOT THE WRONG TYPE OF PLUG THERE.

Your local swimming pool

It would be great if we each had our own swimming pool, but few people do. So, it's usually off to the local town pool for a swim.

Sometimes, pools have several lanes roped off. They may be for club swimmers to practise or they may be reserved for old, disabled or learner swimmers. Some pools these days have water slides called flumes. The really big pools often have wave machines, too. All this can be great fun but to get the most out of such equipment, with safety uppermost, you need to have confidence in the water.

Get ready for fun!

FINDING YOUR WAY AROUND

Even though every pool is different – some have diving
pools, some don't; some are 50 metres in length, others
25 metres – there are many things common to all pools.
The most important of these are the hygiene and safety
features. Do your local pool a big favour by showering
and going to the toilet before swimming,
and by following all safety instructions.

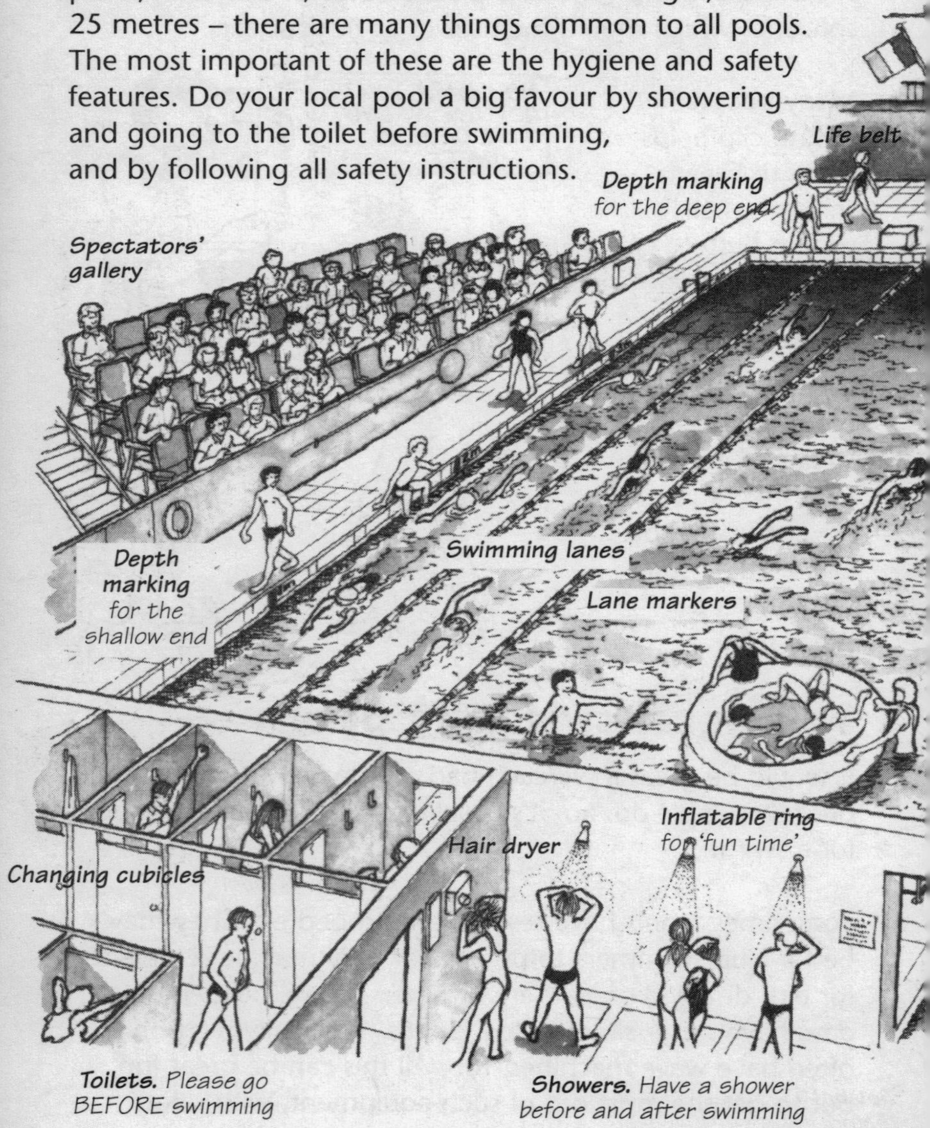

Life belt

Depth marking
for the deep end

Spectators'
gallery

Depth
marking
for the
shallow end

Swimming lanes

Lane markers

Inflatable ring
for 'fun time'

Hair dryer

Changing cubicles

Toilets. Please go
BEFORE swimming

Showers. Have a shower
before and after swimming

Get ready for fun!

The **lifeguard** sits high above the pool so he or she can watch for swimmers in trouble or spot people misbehaving

Clock

High board

Pole used to help troubled swimmers

Springboard

Starting blocks

Diving pool

Swimming instructor

Pool steps

Learners' pool

Foot bath for cleaning feet before entering the pool

Young children can bring swim rings and kickboards into the pool

7

Chlorine power

Chlorine is a necessary evil in public pools. It's a chemical used to prevent infections and keep the pool water clean. Unfortunately, it can sting eyes – that's where goggles come in – and it's also a bleach that can damage your hair and swimsuit if it's not washed out. That's why you should always shower thoroughly after swimming and rinse out your swimsuit and any other equipment with fresh water.

Pool rules OK?

Public pools always have a long list of rules on the walls. Don't ignore them – they're there for the benefit of all swimmers, yes, even you. If using a friend's pool or a pool on holiday, it's still important to follow these rules.

1 Make sure you know where the deep and shallow ends of the pool are.
2 No running jumps or jumping close to other swimmers. Don't bomb-jump other swimmers.
3 Don't jump or dive in backwards. You cannot see what's going on behind you and you may land on someone.
4 Don't duck or splash others. This may destroy their confidence if they are learning to swim.
5 Don't run around the pool. It's easy to slip and crack your head on the hard pool edge.
6 Don't dive in the shallow end. Many pools only allow diving in certain areas. Follow instructions.
7 Look where you're going so you avoid colliding with other swimmers.

Getting confident

If you are new to
swimming, it is quite
natural that you will
be a little nervous.
Remember that
every swimmer
was once a
non-swimmer. Your
family and friends
may have forgotten
this. Remind them
of it. Take your time
in the pool and
learn at your own
pace. Let your
confidence build up
before moving on
to the next stage.

Tips for new swimmers

- Visit swimming pools when they are quiet.
- Use the pool steps to get in and out. Always go down
  with your back to the water.
- Use a swimming aid. The right sort can really help.
- Don't let yourself be teased or bullied into trying new
  things too quickly or before you're really ready.
- Go to the pool between swimming classes with a friend
  who is an experienced swimmer. Practise what you learnt
  in your previous lesson.

9

Getting wet

Jumping in can be dangerous in shallow water. Always check the water is deep enough for your jump beforehand and make sure there is no one near where you intend to jump in.

FEET FIRST DIVE

Used only for jumping into deep water, this is sometimes also known as the straight or pencil jump.

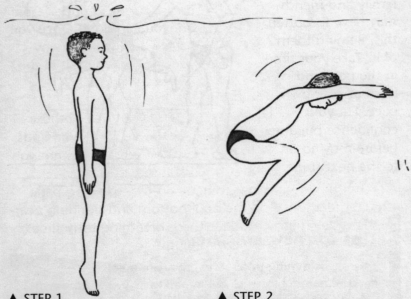

▲ STEP 1
With your arms above your head, jump forward. Keep your body straight and point your toes down. Your arms should come back to your side by the time you enter the water. Aim to make as small a splash as possible.

▲ STEP 2
Once under the water, you can move into a swimming position by drawing your knees up to your chest and leaning forward. Thrusting your legs back, you can then swim an underwater breaststroke (see pages 39-45).

Every breath you take

What bothers many new swimmers most is putting their head underwater. The trouble is, most swimming requires it, so it's best done as early as possible. Ready? Here goes:

Stand in the shallow end and grab firmly hold of the side or pool rail. Close your eyes or wear goggles and duck your head under. Go on, you can do it! Once you have, you'll wonder why you worried about it in the first place.

If you're not one of those lucky so-and-so's who finds breathing when swimming easy, you're going to have to work at it. Start off by practising the breathing technique on the following page with your feet firmly on the pool bottom and standing near the pool side. Then, introduce these breathing techniques gradually into your actual swimming.

Swimming star – David Wilkie

Along with Duncan Goodhew, Sharron Davies and Adrian Moorhouse, Wilkie is the most famous British swimmer. He was the only non-American male gold medal winner in the 1976 Olympics and set a 200m breaststroke record that lasted for more than 10 years.

Get ready for fun!

If you breathe through your nose there's a good chance that water will go up it. That's why breathing in through your mouth is best. A further way to stop water entering your nose is to breathe out through your nose and mouth.

TRICKLE BREATHING

Trickle breathing is when you let your breath out slowly from your nose and mouth when your face is underwater. This means that when you do lift or turn your face out of the water, you are ready to breathe in again.

▲ STEP 1
As your mouth clears the water, take a good-sized breath of air.

▲ STEP 2
Don't gulp or gasp for air. It will spoil your performance.

▲ STEP 3
Let the air slowly trickle out of your nose and mouth as you swim.

◄ STEP 4
Aim to have almost finished one breath out as you want to take one breath in.

STEP 5   ►
Try to get your breathing into a relaxed rhythm.

Swimming aids

Many people make the mistake of thinking floating and swimming aids are only for beginners and young kids. Wrong! They can be very useful in improving swimming generally. Competitive swimmers sometimes use them to brush up on their technique, so why not you? Note, though, that unless you are an absolute beginner, armbands are not helpful when learning swimming strokes.

KICKBOARD
Made of lightweight, buoyant material, they keep you afloat so you can really concentrate on your leg movements.

PULL-BUOY
The pull-buoy is similar to the kickboard, but works the other way round. It fits between your legs and keeps your legs up. This allows you to concentrate on your body and arm movements. Competitive swimmers use pull-buoys as part of their training to develop their hand and arm actions.

FINS
Fins (or flippers) really increase your speed and allow you to concentrate on your arm and body movements. The best fins have a shoe-type fitting rather than just a strap. Fins are usually banned from public pool sessions. However, swimming clubs use them a lot.

2 The science of swimming

Right, let's get going. We'll start by calling on the eminent swimming expert Dr Walter Wingz.

"Thank you, Clive, and hello readers."

"Most human beings are blessed with the ability to float in water. But only just. Our density is a fraction lower than water. This means that we can keep a small part of ourselves above water without moving our arms or legs. Floating can be very useful and, what's more, the face-down float and the back-float are the basis of the main swimming strokes."

Er, thanks, Doc. There you have it – floating is a handy skill. Always practise floating within your depth so you can get your feet down on to the pool bottom with ease.

Swimming star – Dawn Fraser

Three times 100m Olympic freestyle champion, this Australian was the first woman to swim 100m in under a minute.

Floating positions

NATURAL FLOATING POSITION

Find your natural
floating position by
floating face down
in the water. Take a
deep breath, relax
and get your head
under. Try not to move
your arms and legs – just let
them rise or fall naturally. You'll find your
legs will drop down because they're heavy. Your
body, though, should float since your lungs are full of air.

Almost everyone can float in this position. If you can't,
you're probably quite thin. Body fat helps floating. Don't
worry, you can use something called sculling to float with
a minimum of effort, and you can also tread water. There
is more on both these techniques coming up.

STAR FLOAT ON YOUR BACK

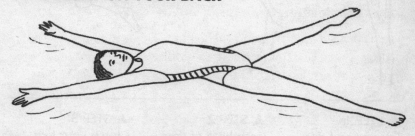

This is the easiest of all floats. The key thing is to prop your
head back quite a long way so your ears are in the water.
Your body will naturally rise to the surface. Use a couple of
kickfloats under your hands if you find it difficult.

FACE-DOWN FLOAT

Lean forward with your
shoulders under the water
and pop your head into
the water. Bring your
arms forward and let
your feet rise up
from the pool floor
until they almost

reach the surface. Move your arms and legs out to the sides
to make a star shape.

MUSHROOM FLOAT

If at first you find the mushroom float a bit tricky, try it with
a kickfloat tucked under each arm.

▲ STEP 1
Take a good deep
breath and float
face down.

▲ STEP 2
Grab hold of your
legs and draw
them up towards
your chest.

▲ STEP 3
Clutch your legs
around the knees.
Hold that position
for a short while
before releasing it.

Touchdown!

You can't float around in the pool forever. At some point, you're going to want to put your feet down and move on.

▲ FRONT FLOAT TOUCHDOWN

From a front float, press down with your arms, lift your head up and bring your knees forward. As you become more upright, push your feet down to the pool floor. Use your arms for balance.

▲ STAR FLOAT TOUCHDOWN

From a star float on your back, lift your head up and scoop around with your arms. Bend your knees and as your body drops down, scoop your hands up in front of you until your feet touch the pool floor.

Synchronised floating anyone?

If you find floating easy, why not combine the flat, star and mushroom floats into your very own synchronised floating routine? There's more on synchronised swimming techniques on pages 95-98.

Sculling

Sculling is a type of hand movement. It can be used to move you through water but is also useful for giving you balance and control when floating.

STATIONARY SUPPORT SCULL

Lying on your back in a floating position, think of your arms as aircraft wings. The leading edge of the wing (your arm) sweeps through the water, back and forth. If you feel your legs sinking, scull more firmly and sweep your hands a little further down towards your feet.

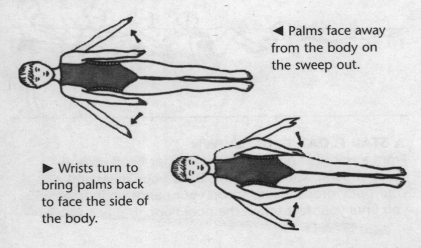

◄ Palms face away from the body on the sweep out.

► Wrists turn to bring palms back to face the side of the body.

MOVING WITH SCULLING

You can use sculling with a back float to move forwards or backwards. The direction will depend on which way your palms are facing. 'Waving goodbye' with your palms facing your feet will cause you to move head-first. Palms facing your head will move you feet-first. In both cases, keep the whole of your hand and wrist under the water.

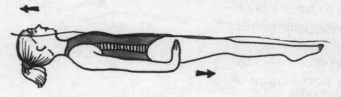

▲ Stick your hands up and push the water away with a waving motion.

▼ Bend your wrists to tilt your hands back with your fingers pointing to the floor of the pool.

Swimming star – Johnny Weissmuller

Your parents will know him as Tarzan in the old films, but before he became a film star Weissmuller was the best technical swimmer in the world. His graceful and powerful style inspired many others. Amazingly, he never lost a race and broke an astonishing 67 world records in distances from 45m to 800m.

FIGURE-OF-EIGHT SCULL

This is a more complicated sculling technique that offers precise movement. It is used a lot by synchronised swimmers.

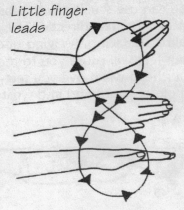

Little finger leads

You need to trace a figure-of-eight with your hands. Keep your fingers together and rotate your wrists to make the whole figure-of-eight movement.

Wrist bends as hand traces figure-of-eight shape through water

Hands scull close to body and legs

Relax

When sculling or treading water keep your leg, arm and breathing movements as relaxed as possible. Your legs and arms should move gently but continuously. As a fun exercise, practise moving from a back float to treading water and back again.

Treading water

Treading water is a top skill to have under your belt for several reasons. Staying still with a minimum of effort like this is vital for survival skills, handy for water polo and other water sports, and is a great way of being able just to stop, take a breather and have a look round. All swimmers should be able to tread water.

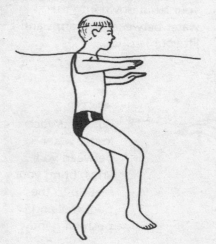

Keep your body upright and hold your head just above the surface of the water. Your chin should be just brushing the water's surface. Keep your arms under the water for balance and use your hands and arms to move water down and away from you. Practise treading water until you can stay in the same position for one minute.

You have a choice of movements for your legs. You can either do a gentle breaststroke leg kick (see pages 28-29) or you can pedal an imaginary underwater bicycle. What? Yes, imagine you're on a bike and pedal it slowly in the water.

Swimming to survive

Swimming for fun is a relatively recent notion. For ancient civilisations, swimming was an important survival skill. It let them cross rivers in order to hunt, find new land or to flee disaster.

Let's get moving

PUSH AND GLIDE

◄ STEP 1

With your back to the pool wall, bend your knees and place your arms out in front of you flat in the water. Duck your head down into the water between your arms and lift your legs up.

◄ STEP 2

With your face in the water between your arms, bring your feet up to the pool wall and push off gently.

▲ STEP 3

Hold the position on top of the water until you feel yourself stopping. To glide further, stand closer to the wall and push off with more power.

PUSH AND GLIDE ON YOUR BACK

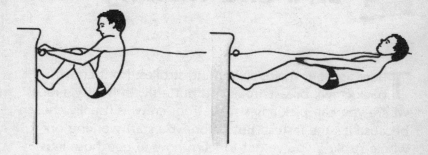

▲ STEP 1
Stand facing the side of the pool with your hands gripping the side. Bring your knees up to your chest with your feet against the pool wall.

▲ STEP 2
Push off smoothly but firmly and lie back. You will find yourself gliding away from the pool wall. Ask a friend to keep your gliding path clear.

▲ STEP 3
This is the basic glide position. Once you are confident, you can get more distance by bringing your arms up and around your head so that they are stretched out above your head and lying flat in the water.

3 Live and kicking

There are four major swimming strokes: front crawl, back crawl, breaststroke and butterfly. In freestyle races where you can pick any stroke, front crawl is usually chosen because it's the fastest. But before you start working on whole strokes, you've got to learn how to get those legs moving. So in this chapter, it's time to get kicking!

SPEED OF STROKES

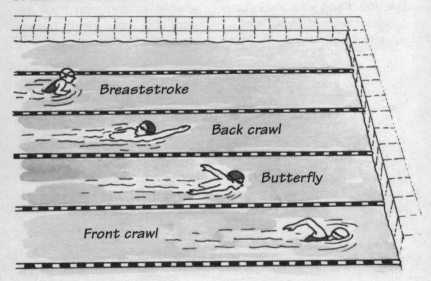

Surprisingly, your legs don't provide most of the power in front crawl, back crawl and butterfly. So why bother with fancy leg work? Because by moving your legs correctly you keep your body streamlined and balanced as you perform the rest of the stroke.

Front crawl kick

The front crawl or flutter kick is an alternate up and down movement of your legs. The power comes from you driving strongly as each leg moves down through the water. Point your toes and stretch your feet.

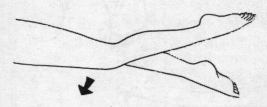

Legs whip through the water almost straight, but not stiff

Keep kick under water. At most, heels should break the surface

▲ Always kick from your hips using your whole leg, and not from your knees. Kicking only from your knees loses you power and makes you less balanced and streamlined. These all add up to slower progress through the water.

▲ Practise the kick by holding on to the pool side and extending your arms. Lock your arms, fully-extended. Try, also to get your head under the water.

Your legs have to kick well to move you forward

Kickboard creates drag

▲ A kickboard gives you buoyancy that lets you concentrate on your leg movements. Holding the kickboard as shown is a useful resistance exercise.

Back crawl kick

This is similar to the front crawl kick, but turned over. Keep your legs stretched out with your feet pointed. Try to turn your toes inwards. This helps them act as paddles and is called intoeing.

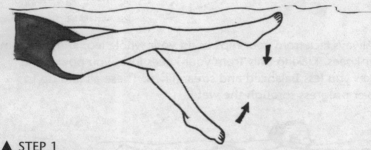

▲ STEP 1
At the end of the downbeat, your leg is below your body, lower than with a front crawl kick.

▲ STEP 2
Don't kick too deeply. The low leg position will slow you down.

▲ STEP 3
The upbeat of the back crawl kick provides lots of power.

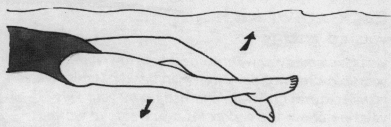

▲ STEP 4

Push the water up and off the top of your foot, letting the toes just break the surface. Knees stay just below the water at all times.

Dolphin kick

Used in the butterfly stroke, your legs stay together and move together throughout the kick. The kick starts from the hips with your heels just breaking the surface of the water. Keep your hips high to maintain the correct body position.

▶ STEP 1

Your lower legs whip down as your legs straighten. Keep your legs together with your toes pointed. Try to keep your ankles flexible.

▶ STEP 2

On the way up, your legs are straight until halfway towards the surface. Then, your knees bend, bringing your lower legs up so that your heels break the surface.

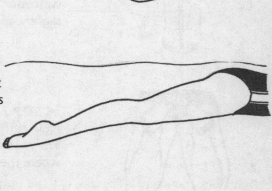

Wasted energy

As a swimmer you want to be as energy efficient as possible. One hot tip is to remember that white water (the splashes and froth churned up by your legs kicking above the surface) is a sure sign of wasted effort. Keep your legs and feet working as much below the water as possible.

Whip kick

Used in breaststroke, the whip kick looks more complicated than it actually is! Though it may take time to perfect, it's worth the effort. Here are the basics, but there is more on how to improve your whip kick in chapter 5.

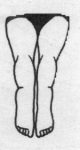

◄ STEP 1
Start off by drawing your heels up towards your bottom with your knees bent and slightly apart.

◄ STEP 2
Now comes the crucial part. The next stage, the drive, is where the power comes from.

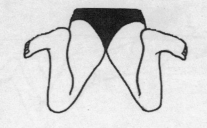

◀ STEP 3

Your feet turn outwards as you drive your legs out and backwards. This gives you maximum power. Try to push your hips up at the same time.

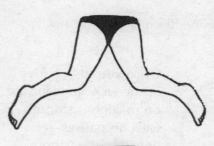

◀ STEP 4

The drive ends with your legs fully extended. Turn your feet so that your soles point up as you bring your legs together.

◀ STEP 5

Sweep your legs back in to get your legs back to the beginning of the kick.

Swimming star – Captain Matthew Webb

It was a long time ago, but for a swimming feat of daring, Captain Webb's successful first crossing of the English Channel in 1875 takes some beating. The experts said it was impossible but Webb proved them wrong, swimming 63 kilometres (39 miles) in 21 hours and 45 minutes.

Live and kicking

The whip kick needs plenty of practice. One exercise is to place a kickboard under each arm so you can concentrate just on the kick.

Body position for the whip kick

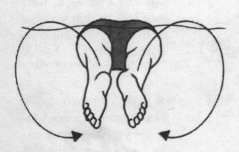

Circular heel movement

Once you get an idea of the kick, concentrate on making it smooth with no pauses between the various stages. A good whip kick action has your heels moving in a circular motion.

Four-stroke engine

As a swimmer, try to be a four-stroke engine. It's more interesting to learn all of the strokes, and overall you'll become a better swimmer. Over time, you may find you have a particularly strong stroke that you want to concentrate on. That's fine, but don't forget to swim the other strokes. They add variety and fun to your swimming.

4 Front crawl

The fastest stroke and the one you've most probably already attempted. Even if you think you're handy at the front crawl, your technique could probably do with some brushing up.

BASIC BODY POSITION
Your basic body position should be as flat as possible with your hips just below the surface and your shoulders resting on the water's surface. Your eyes look forward and down.

Part of your face should stay in the water at all times, even when you're breathing

Legs stretched out with

Turn your toes in

Fingers stay close together

Think of a line running right through the middle of you. You want to keep all parts of your body, arms and legs as close to this centre line as possible. By keeping your whole self straight and by making yourself as narrow as possible, you will cut through the water with greater speed.

Swimming star – Tracy Caulkins

Tracy Caulkins was an incredible swimmer from the United States who was world-ranked in each of the four individual strokes. She won three Olympic golds in Olympic medley competitions where all four strokes have to be swimmed.

JUST THE ONE

To start, let's go through one arm cycle for the front crawl first.

◄ STEP 1
Slide your right arm into the water with your elbow high. Your hand should enter the water just inside your shoulder line.

◄ STEP 2
Start to bend your right elbow as your arm pulls down and back through the water.

▶ STEP 3
Push your right arm back and up towards your hip.

▶ STEP 4
Lift your right arm out of the water elbow first. The palm of your hand should be facing your thigh. This is the start of the recovery stroke.

▶ STEP 5
Keeping your elbow high, bring your right arm over your body and back into the water to start the stroke all over again.

Resisting resistance

Jet planes have pointed noses so that they can cut through the air with as little resistance as possible. Resistance is a kind of friction caused by an object moving through air or water. It slows the object down. In swimming, you can cut resistance and improve streamlining by wearing a fitting swimsuit and by adopting a good swimming position.

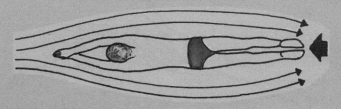

SECOND-ARM CYCLE

Now, let's add the second-arm cycle into the crawl stroke. The front view pictures show how your body must roll from side to side. You roll your shoulders towards the hand

SIDE VIEW
STEP 1

STEP 2

STEP 3

STEP 4

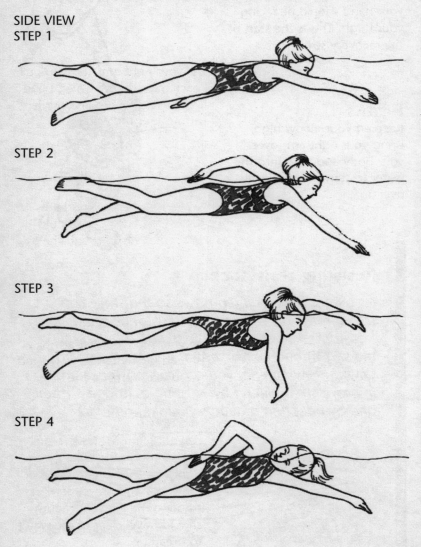

entering the water. After that hand has pulled through the water, and your other hand is entering the water, you start to roll to the other side. The roll should be gentle and smooth. Try not to lurch from side to side.

FRONT VIEW

◀ STEP 1

As your right arm starts to pull back through the water, bend your left elbow to lift your left arm out of the water.

◀ STEP 2

As your right arm continues its stroke, your left arm should move forward through the air.

◀ STEP 3

As your right arm pushes back to your hip, your left arm should slide into the water and your head turns to the side.

◀ STEP 4

As your left arm starts to pull back through the water, your right arm should lift up out of the water and move forward through the air. Your mouth should travel clear of the water to breath.

The kick

As your arms perform the stroke, your legs should be kicking. (The flutter kick is shown on page 25.) Don't pummel your legs up and down – kick smoothly but firmly – concentrating on starting the kick from the hip. Good swimmers aim for a total of six leg kicks for every complete arm cycle, that's three kicks of each leg each time one hand completes its stroke through the water, recovers through the air and enters the water again.

S-PULLS
Best shown in a picture, this is the way your hand and arm should move as you make a stroke.

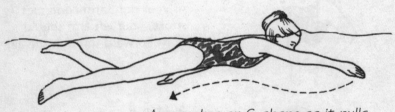

Arm makes an S-shape as it pulls through the water

Swimming star – Duke Kahanamoku

Hawaiian swimming star, Duke Kahanamoku, won Olympic freestyle gold medals in 1912 and 1920. He helped change the front crawl technique to the style used today.

Breathe easily

Your body roll is the basis of your breathing position. As you roll to one side, turn your head the opposite way, as if you were a pirate talking to a parrot on your shoulder. No, really, it works! This should place your mouth above the water so you can take a breath. Breathing out is mainly done underwater.

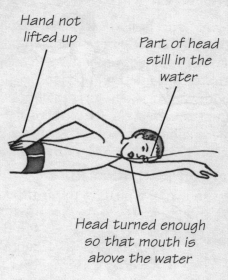

Hand not lifted up

Part of head still in the water

Head turned enough so that mouth is above the water

At first, it's fine to pick just one side to breathe on and take a breath in every arm cycle on that side. But as you improve, you may want to try bilateral breathing. This is when you take a breath first from one side and then from the other side. Top swimmers breathe every third, fifth or seventh stroke!

TURN AND TURN AGAIN

Congratulations – you can swim the front crawl. Or at least you are well on your way to swimming the front crawl with a lot of style and speed. The better you get at it, the faster the end of the pool will appear, presenting another challenge – just what is the best way to turn around? Swimming turns for crawl and the other strokes are dealt with in chapter 12.

Front crawl fault finder

LEGS DROPPING?
The most likely reason is your head is high out of the water as if you're doing a doggy paddle. Get your head back into the water!

TOO MUCH BODY ROLL

This will spoil your stroke rhythm. You may be pulling too deep with your arms, but more likely is that you're over-reaching. This means that your hand is reaching too far across your body before it enters the water. Practise the stroke, concentrating on getting your hand to enter the water along the centre line.

RECOVERY ARM TOO HIGH
This will slow you down. Practise the stroke, lifting your elbow to recover with an outward swing. Think of removing your hand from a deep trouser pocket. That's the correct arm action!

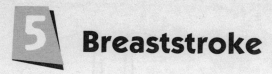

Breaststroke

Breaststroke is a very useful stroke. Not only is it a great competitive stroke by itself, but it's also the business for swimming underwater.

We have already looked at the leg action for breaststroke and here we concentrate on the basic body position, the movement of the arms – and the all-important putting together of all the ingredients into one seemingly effortless and very elegant swimming stroke.

Turn back to the previous chapter for a refresher on the whip kick; you have to get this right to be a successful breaststroke swimmer. Work on it by holding a kickboard and try to do widths of the pool using only the leg action.

Arm movements

From below, the arm movement looks a lot like a heart shape. Both arms move at the same time and in the same way. But it's not just a flat sweep of the arms. Your hands push forward together and then pull around in a circular motion until they finish back under your chest.

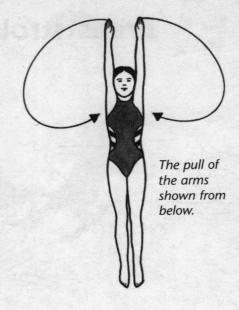

The pull of the arms shown from below.

▼ STEP 1

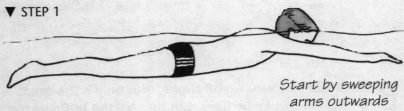

Start by sweeping arms outwards

▼ STEP 2

Head rises

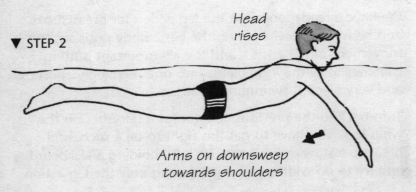

Arms on downsweep towards shoulders

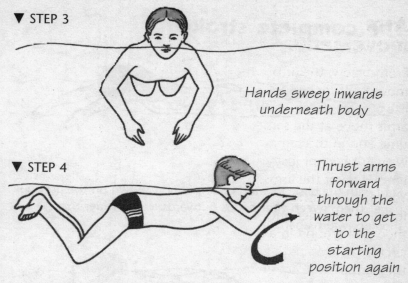

▼ STEP 3

Hands sweep inwards
underneath body

▼ STEP 4

Thrust arms
forward
through the
water to get
to the
starting
position again

Remember, your elbows should stay under the water throughout the stroke. A simple tip is to imagine your arms as three animals. First, an elephant with the trunk extended, then a monkey with the arms bent and pulling, and finally, as a mouse with your hands underneath your chin.

Practise the arm action by walking it through. Get your shoulders under the water and lean forwards to simulate the breaststroke position. Slowly walk forwards while you perform just the arm stroke.

Basic body position

Your body should be fairly flat just under the water with your arms around your ears and your hands together. Your legs and hips should be a little lower than your body and your head a little higher so that you are looking forward with your chin on or just in the water.

The complete stroke

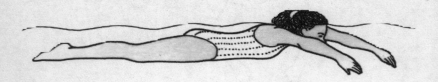

▲ STEP 1

Start with the basic forward glide position shown on the previous page. Then, sweep your hands outwards a little wider than shoulder-width apart.

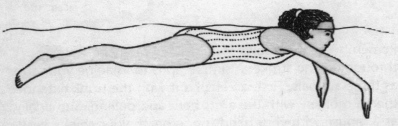

▲ STEP 2

Well before your arms reach your shoulders, turn your hands so your palms face back with your fingers pointing down.

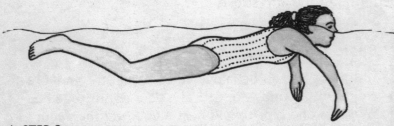

▲ STEP 3

Pull out, down and back firmly. Your elbows must stay high but bend sharply. You should start to lift your head and shoulders forwards and up.

▲ STEP 4

When your hands pass below your elbows, sweep your hands in, palms facing each other. As you do this, start your kick by bringing your heels up towards your bottom.

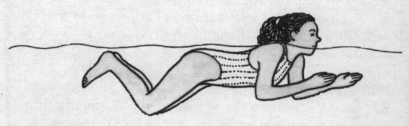

▲ STEP 5

As your hands come beneath your chin, you will find your head rising above the water. Now is the time to take a breath. At the same time drive your legs back with your feet turned out.

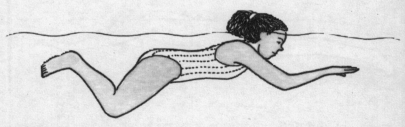

▲ STEP 6

Thrust your arms out in front of you as you complete the kick. As you finish the kick, your toes should be facing backwards and your arms should be ahead of you as you glide forward, ready for the next stroke.

Breaststroke tips

RHYTHM AND TIMING

Absolutely vital to breaststroke, rhythm and timing only come from swimming distances. A simple tip is to think pull-kick-glide. Pull with the arms, kick with the legs and glide along, before starting the next stroke.

BREATHING

Compared to the other strokes, it's easy. The shape of the stroke naturally moves your head up and out of the water. Breathe in as your arms pull back through the water. Breathe out as the arms stretch forwards. Breathe between each stroke cycle.

PRACTICE MAKES PERFECT

You need to get both the arm and leg movements right for breaststroke to work. If you are having problems, you can split up the arm and leg movements and practise them separately. Push and glide from the pool wall and attempt just arm or leg actions for a while.

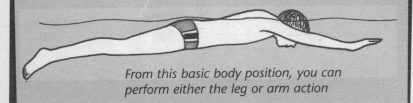

From this basic body position, you can perform either the leg or arm action

Many of the difficulties you may face with breaststroke involve getting the arms and legs to work together. The fault finder guide on the next page offers solutions to some of the most common problems.

Breaststroke fault finder

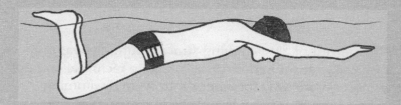

HEAD TOO LOW
If your feet break the surface of the water all the time there's every chance your head is too low. Practise your kicking action while blowing across the surface of the water. If you can't blow, your head's too low!

HEAD TOO HIGH
This will cause your hips and legs to sink too low in the water, slowing you down. Concentrate on keeping your chin touching the surface of the water.

ARMS PULLING TOO WIDE
This stops you lifting your head to breathe. It also mucks up the timing of your leg and arm strokes. Practise the arm movement standing up, thinking especially about bending your elbows and squeezing in.

SCREW KICKING
This very common fault is caused by twisted hips or shoulders, or dropping one knee lower than the other – basically, anything which stops you lying flat in the water. Always look straight ahead – your body and legs will follow. One exercise is to hold a kickboard and focus on it while practising your kick.

6 Butterfly

The newest of all swimming strokes, butterfly was only officially recognised in 1952. It's quite technical and not the most natural way for a person to swim. Swimming teachers tend to teach it last of the four strokes so you don't see it that often in a busy swimming pool. Imagine being the first of your swimming friends to get to grips with it. Boy, will you look cool!

Swimming star – Mark Spitz

This incredibly talented American swimmer had already bagged one previous gold in the 1968 Olympics. His tally of seven swimming gold medals in the 1972 Olympics for freestyle, butterfly and team relays is unlikely ever to be equalled.

THINK DOLPHIN!

The butterfly stroke requires you to combine three elements: the arm movement (shown on pages 48-49) and the dolphin kick with a flexible body position. In short, your body has to undulate.

Undulation is a gentle, wave-like movement through your body. It's what dolphins do when they swim underwater. You want to do the same as your body moves from a level, streamlined position to one where your hips rise and your legs trail down at an angle.

Keep your body as streamlined as possible as you move

See the way your body bends gently

Throughout the stroke, your hips rise and fall but your bottom should not stick out of the water at any time.

You have to keep the undulations gentle. Too vigorous and your body and head will launch high out of the water or plough deep underwater, both of which will slow you down. Keep as flat a body position as is possible with the stroke. That way you will slice through the water more quickly.

The complete stroke

FRONT VIEW

◀ STEP 1 ▶

Your hands enter the water, fingers first, about shoulder-width apart. They should be angled a little with your palms facing outwards. Your arms are not quite fully stretched out ahead of you and your head is in the water.

◀ STEP 2 ▶

Tilt your hands with the palms facing back and move your arms outwards with elbows bent so your hands are well wide of your shoulders.

◀ STEP 3 ▶

Your hands now sweep back and inwards pressing on the water and forcing it back with power. Your head now starts to rise and your hips drop.

SIDE VIEW

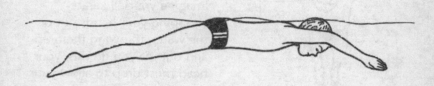

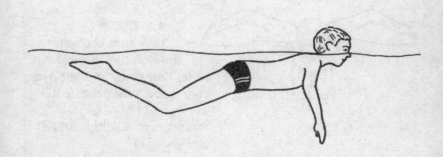

Butterfly

FRONT VIEW

◀ STEP 4 ▶
Push your hands back to your thighs. As you push with your hands, push your chin forwards. This should get your mouth clear of the water for you to take a breath.

◀ STEP 5 ▶
Imagine yourself karate-chopping your hands out of the water, throwing them up and out. As you do this, your head must drop to allow your shoulders to rotate to bring your arms over.

◀ STEP 6 ▶
Your arms recover through the air. Held out wide, they come straight over your body. Your hands enter the water in front of your shoulders to start the stroke all over again.

SIDE VIEW

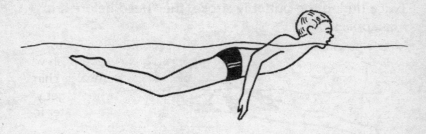

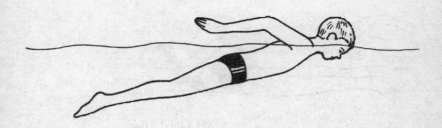

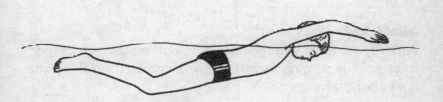

Butterfly

HEAD BEFORE ARMS
Twice during the butterfly stroke, the "head before arms" rule applies.

▲ FIRST TIME:
Your head should lift out of the water before your arms do.

▲ SECOND TIME:
When your arms are out of the water and swinging forward, your head should enter the water before your arms do.

ARMS AND LEGS
Butterfly relies on you moving your legs and arms together to create the surging forward movement. Getting this right is all about timing.

There are two complete dolphin kicks for each arm stroke. The first kick starts down as your arms enter the water. The second should occur just as your arms complete their pull and start to leave the water. Swimming coaches say, "Kick your arms in and kick your arms out."

Butterfly tips and fault finder

KEEP IT SHORT

Butterfly swimming is the most tiring stroke for most people. Don't put yourself under too much pressure when practising. At first, look to do two or three strokes before stopping. Gradually, build up the distance you can swim butterfly.

FAST FIN FUN

Fins give you more power from the kick while you're learning butterfly. You can practise the dolphin kick on your front, on your back or even underwater. Whenever using fins with the dolphin kick, always lead with your arms out in front of you.

TIMING TIP

Push and glide then perform four complete leg kicks to one complete arm pull. This gives you time to think about the arm movements. Look to reduce the number of kicks per arm cycle to three and then two.

ONE-ARM ACTION

With one arm in front of you in the glide position, perform the butterfly arm movement with the other arm. Keep the dolphin kick going throughout your practice session.

7 Back crawl

Tip number one: practise this stroke in plenty of space. Or have a lookout who can keep your way clear. At first, looking round is inevitable, but as you get more confident you'll need to less and less. You can still make sure you are on the straight and narrow by learning to pick spots on the ceiling or the wall you are swimming away from. Going in a straight line really is vital with this one! Get that sorted and you're on your way.

BASIC BODY POSITION

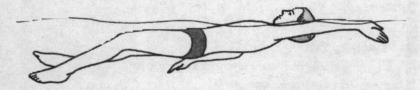

Your body position should be almost horizontal with the back of your head and your ears just below the water. Ideally, your eyes should be looking up and slightly back towards your feet and your stomach should be up, helping to lift your hips. Your legs should be slightly lower than your body. This helps keep your kick under the water.

One-arm action

Let's go through one complete arm cycle.

◀ STEP 1

Your hand enters the water, little finger first, with your palm facing outwards. Your fingers are together. Your hand enters the water in front of your head and in line with, or just wide of, your shoulder.

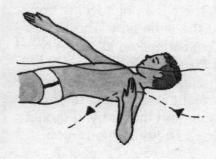

◀ STEP 2

Your shoulder drops letting your hand sink about 30cm underwater. Keep your arm straight but bend your wrist toward your little finger. You should now start to 'feel' the water against your hand.

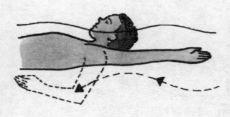

◀ STEP 3

Think of your arm pulling on a rope. Sweep your arm up, then down as if it was compressing a giant spring. Your elbow will bend and drop, but don't let it just slip through the water. You should feel the pressure of the water on your hand all the time.

Hand rotates so that little finger leads

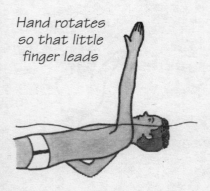

◀ STEP 4

Your hand leaves the water thumb first. You lift your arm straight and vertically, carrying it clear of the water. As your arm recovers through the air, turn your palm outwards so that your hand re-enters the water little finger first.

One arm good, two arms better

Now let's add the second arm. The back crawl involves alternate arm strokes. As one arm recovers out of the water, the other arm performs an S-pull firmly through the water.

Because it takes less time to move your arm through the air than it does through the water, there is a point where both of your arms are in the water at the same time. This is the point where your left arm has just completed its recovery through the air and is entering the water and your right arm is just finishing its S-pull through the water. As your arm recovers, it should be as straight and as close to your side as possible. As the top of your arm travels by, it should just brush your ear. If it does, you're getting things right.

Coaches advise you to think of the end of one arm stroke pushing the other arm in and through the water.

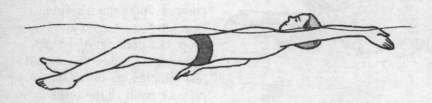

▲ STEP 1 ▶
Hand enters the water with the fingers pointed and palm facing away from the body.

▲ STEP 2 ▶
Hand sweeps out and up. Other
arm starts to rise through the air.

▲ STEP 3 ▶
Elbow straightens as hand forces
water away. Other arm windmills
through the air.

Back crawl

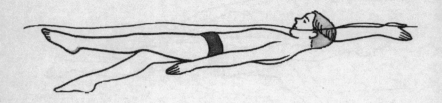

▲ STEP 4 ▶

As the arm under the water finishes its stroke, the hand of the other arm should enter the water.

▲ STEP 5 ▶

Arm leaves the water and starts to recover through the air. Aim for six leg kicks for every complete cycle of the stroke. Remember, your legs move fast while your arms move slowly.

58

BREATHING

Breathing is pretty straightforward with the back crawl because your mouth is always out of the water. Try to breathe regularly, timing your breaths so that you breathe in as one arm comes out of the water and breathe out as the other arm recovers.

BACK CRAWL S-PULL

This is the hardest element to describe. Try to practise the S-pull with an expert onlooker to comment on your style.

1 Elbow bends and drops as the shoulder rolls towards your arm.
2 Keep your forearm at about right angles to your upper arm.
3 Pull your arm in a curve towards the surface of the water.
4 As hand reaches your shoulder, the pull becomes a push.
5 Your hand pushes down in a curve to just beneath your thigh. Your shoulders start to lift ready for the final stage.

DON'T LOOK NOW

Try to keep your head as still as possible. Sure, your body rolls from side to side with each arm stroke, but your head should remain as flat and as level in the water as possible. This gives you a more streamlined shape.

Back crawl tips

ARM PRACTICE

Remember the pull-buoy? Well, here's a grand opportunity to use it. Gripping the pull-buoy between your thighs keeps your legs floating and your hips close to the surface. The pull-buoy helps you get the correct body position and allows you to work on your arms.

SIMPLE PULL

If you're new to the back crawl or are struggling with the S-pull underwater, try out this simpler arm pull.

The arm recovers and enters the water as on the proper stroke, but here's the difference. Turn your hand outwards as you make a shallow side sweep with your arm straight down towards your hips.

Because of water resistance, you will find it almost impossible to keep a completely straight arm. Your arm naturally bends as it encounters the weight of the water. The good news is that the way your arm bends is the start of the S-pull stroke.

8 Fit to swim

Swimming is a demanding sport. A competitive swimmer's regular training programme is a mixture of different swimming exercises and other disciplines. Top swimmers pay attention to their diet and spend almost as much time in the gym as they do in the pool.

If you're serious about your swimming, you should join a swimming club and talk to an experienced coach about constructing your own training programme.

STRETCHING THE POINT

A training programme will include a lot of flexibility exercises making you really supple and giving you easy movement in all joints.

Swimming uses more muscle groups than most sports. It's important that the key muscles are stretched before swimming. Stretching gets the muscles ready for exercise and helps reduce the chance of muscle strains or leg cramps. Seek advice from swimmers or a good coach about the many different stretching exercises available.

Strong sides

The muscles on the sides of your body are vital for the rolling motion of the front and back crawls. Here's one of a number of different side stretches you can do.

▲ STEP 1
With one hand on your hip and legs a little apart, lift the other arm above your head from your side and bend sideways until you feel your side muscles pulling.

▲ STEP 2
Hold this position and then return slowly to the upright position. Repeat, bending to the other side. Do ten of these stretches.

Energy food

A good diet will give you plenty of energy for your swimming without you putting on weight. Try to eat lots of fresh fruit and vegetables and other foods that are high in carbohydrates such as cereal, pasta, fish and lean chicken.

Bolder shoulders

Your shoulders provide most of your arm power. And in most strokes, it's your arms that drive you forward when swimming far more than your legs. So, it makes sense to have your shoulders in tip top condition. Right? Thought you'd agree.

▼ Swing one arm slowly in as large a circle as possible, forwards for ten circles, then backwards. Repeat with the other arm.

▲ Stand straight with your legs slightly apart and your knees flexed. Bring one arm over and behind your head to touch the middle of your back. Hold your elbow with your other hand and gently push your hand further down your back. Do this five times then repeat with the other arm.

63

Loose legs

EXERCISE 1 ▶
You need a towel for this excellent
leg stretch. Position yourself
near a wall and hook
the towel over your
feet. Rock back on
your bottom so that
the wall supports your
back. Aim to create as
large an arc with your feet
as possible.

EXERCISE 2 ▶
Find a piece of dry, non-slippery
floor next to a wall. Keeping
your heels on the floor, bend
forward and with your
arms at full stretch, place
the palms of your
hands flat on to the
wall. This exercise
should safely
stretch your
leg muscles.

Safe sport

*Swimming is one of the safest sports around. When top
competition swimmers are unable to compete, it is
often because of a training injury incurred out of the
pool. Always shower after swimming and wrap up
warm. You don't want to catch a chill or cold which
will impair your breathing.*

Looking after yourself

GENTLY DOES IT

If you're looking to do a long-distance swim or some sprints, work up to it. Do some gentle swimming first to warm you up and to get your arms, legs, heart and lungs ready for the exercise ahead. A good tip is to do some gentle lengths or widths of the pool using a different stroke from the one you intend working on.

SWIMMER'S EYE

Chlorine in public pools can irritate the eyes. Get a bottle of eye-drops. Apply a drop in each eye after swimming to soothe them.

SWIMMER'S EAR

Minor ear infections can occur if your ears aren't thoroughly dried after swimming. Ear plugs can help, but if you do get earache, use alcohol-based ear drops. If the problem persists, see your doctor.

SWIMMER'S SHOULDER

Sore shoulders are the most likely ache you will get from swimming. There is no real cure other than lots of rest. When you next swim, take it gently.

SWIMMER'S CRAMPS

Cramps in your lower leg are caused by a lack of blood reaching the muscle at the right time. The most likely causes are a very tight swimsuit, a blow to the muscle or sudden muscle exertion.

If you get a cramp, get out of the water. Usually, gently stretching the muscle solves the problem. If it persists, loosen the muscle with some gentle massage and wrap your leg in a dry towel.

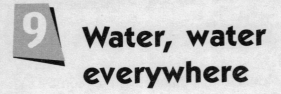

9 Water, water everywhere

Swimming in rivers, lakes or the sea is known as open-water swimming. Open-water swimming can be terrific fun, but there are risks and you must be fully aware of them.

Every year, about 650 people drown in the United Kingdom. All bar a couple of these terrible deaths occur in open water.

In difficulties

If you find yourself in difficulties, first and most important, KEEP CALM! If you can do this, you're going to be fine. Remember, you can float, especially if you're in sea water which supports you more than fresh water. Gently tread water if you're uncomfortable floating. Try to use as little energy as possible.

Get your energy and confidence back and gently swim back to safety. If you need help, shout and wave an arm. Otherwise, just stay calm and slowly swim. A good swimming style for this – because it is not as tiring as front crawl – is the side stroke.

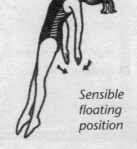

Sensible floating position

Open water swimming

THE TEN COMMANDMENTS

1 Never fool around near water.
2 Never swim in open water until you are a competent swimmer in a pool.
3 Never swim alone.
4 Never swim in rivers or in the sea where there is a strong current.
5 Never jump, dive or swim in water where you cannot see the bottom.
6 Never swim near boats or in areas roped off for water-skiing, jet skis or high-diving.
7 Never swim near piers or breakwaters.
8 Always follow notices and flags which show you where or where not to swim.
9 Always swim parallel to the shore when in the sea, not straight out. Keep a constant eye on the nearest land.
10 Be aware of your temperature. If you start feeling cold, get out of the water. Cold shock can be harmful. Be especially aware of lakes and rivers which can be extremely cold even in summer.

Side stroke

This ancient stroke is useful out in open water, especially if you are tired or cold.

◀ STEP 1
Your starting position is on your side with the side of your head in the water and your eyes and nose just above the surface. Your legs scissor kick one above the other. In the gliding part of the stroke, your arms are stretched out, one leading ahead of you, the other flat by your side.

◀ STEP 2
From the stretched glide position (pic.1) The leading arm pulls, as the arm by the side recovers to the chest and the legs split open.

◀ STEP 3
As the leading arm recovers, the arm alongside the chest pushes back to the hips and the legs scissor together back to the stretched glide position of picture 1.

Lifesaving

If you see someone in trouble in the water, stay calm. Shout for help, alert a lifeguard if one is nearby and, if there's a group of you, send someone to get help quickly.

Don't get in the water yourself. Two people in difficulty is far worse than one. If the person is near the edge of the water, lie down flat and offer a stick or piece of clothing for them to grab. Hold on to something secure or if someone else is with you, get them to hold on to you.

If you can't reach the person, throw a swimming aid such as a float or life-ring into the water for them to hold on to.

LEARNING LIFESAVING

Every year, a quarter of a million people in Britain take part in lifesaving training. It's an enjoyable and valuable thing to learn and it improves your swimming abilities. There are even lifesaving competitions. If you're interested in learning about lifesaving, contact your local swimming pool for details of classes.

Distance swimming

For distance, read long distance. This is swimming for people with staying power! Any swimming competition more than 1500m is considered a distance event. Most distance races are between six and 20 kilometres (3.7 to 12.4 miles), though there are a few gut-busting events like the 80km (50-mile) Lake Michigan Endurance Swim in the United States.

I SAID IT WOULD BE A TREK, BUT I DID'NT MEAN YOU TO BRING A WALKING STICK

Much long-distance swimming takes place in open water. Often the swimmers have to face hazards such as currents, waves and even jellyfish stings. Some distance swimmers around the coast of Florida swim inside a metal cage dragged by a motor boat to protect them from sharks!

Grease!

Swimming in open water can be a very chilly experience. Long distance swimmers wear special insulated swimsuits and extra-thick caps, sometimes two of them. Most cover themselves with a mixture of oils and lotions including petroleum jelly for warmth and a strong sun block. This is known as greasing up.

Crossing the Channel

Swimming the English Channel has become a popular challenge. In 1926, 19-year-old American Gertrude Ederle became the first woman to make the crossing, recording a time of 14 hours, 30 minutes. Since then, men and women as young as 12 and as old as 65 have swum the Channel. The current record is a speedy seven hours, 17 minutes.

Triathlon swimming

Distance swimming is found in another popular sport, the triathlon. Triathlons are a three-stage event incorporating long-distance swimming along with cycling and running. In a typical triathlon, competitors first swim 1500m, then cycle 40km (25 miles) and finally complete a 10km (6.5 mile) run. Absolutely exhausting!

Underwater swimming

If you've done the push and glide properly, you've already swum a little underwater. Now, you can go a little further. Keep your eyes open to see where you're going. Remember, as with all swimming, make sure you've mastered the moves in a pool before trying them out in open water.

UNDERWATER STROKE

Because water is harder than air to move through, strokes like butterfly and front crawl, which rely on you whipping your arms over your head, are almost impossible underwater. Use the breaststroke, with either a proper breaststroke kick or a front crawl kick.

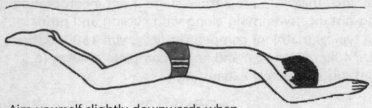

▲ Aim yourself slightly downwards when you swim underwater. This is to allow for your natural tendency to float to the surface. Don't forget to look where you are going!

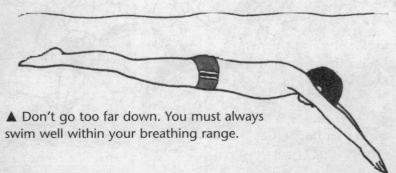

▲ Don't go too far down. You must always swim well within your breathing range.

SURFACE DIVE

Take a deep breath and stretch out on your front. Pull your arms sharply round and back like you would in breaststroke, but at the same time thrust your head and shoulders down into the water and bend at the waist.

As your legs start to come out of the water, straighten your hips and push your legs up into the air so they are straight. Push your arms forward until they're stretched out in front of you and round your head. You'll find yourself sinking below the water. Don't kick your legs until they're under the water.

If you want to go deeper, make another breaststroke pull with your arms.

To go from this near-vertical position to a horizontal one, turn your fingers up.

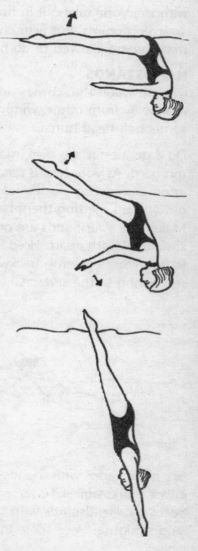

73

Underwater fun

You can have brilliant fun underwater, especially if there is a group of you in the pool. What about staging your own underwater Olympics? This works best with handstands, with everyone taking it in turns to do one and the rest awarding points. But first: check with the pool lifeguard that you are allowed to do handstands.

HANDSTANDS

Choose water that comes up to your shoulder and keep well away from other swimmers. A leg landing on someone's head hurts!

Do a gentle surface dive, making sure you don't drive down too hard. As your hands reach the bottom, tuck yourself into a bunny hop position. From this, you can kick your legs out and up, getting them to rise above the water's surface. Make sure your hands are on the pool bottom about shoulder-width apart. Hold for a short while before letting your legs drop backwards and recovering to the surface.

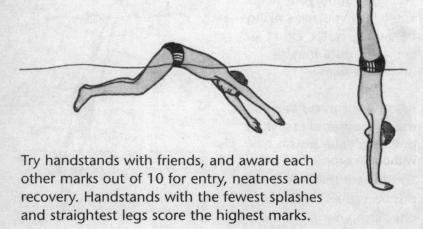

Try handstands with friends, and award each other marks out of 10 for entry, neatness and recovery. Handstands with the fewest splashes and straightest legs score the highest marks.

Front somersault

▲ STEP 1
Round your back and tuck
your knees up to your chest.

▲ STEP 2
With your arms away from
your sides, drop your head
and start to turn down and
round.

▲ STEP 3
Use your hands to sweep the
water backwards. It's a little
like skipping backwards but
without the rope. This helps
your body turn forwards and
over. You'll soon find yourself
face up.

▲ STEP 4
From here, continue
sweeping, but unbend your
legs to get them down on
to the pool floor.

Backward somersault

▲ STEP 1
Draw your knees up to your chest and tuck your chin in. Push down with your hands.

▲ STEP 2
Pull your knees over your head, and rotate your arms as if skipping forwards.

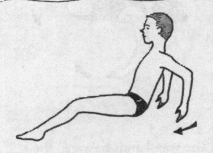

▲ STEP 3
Use your hands to sweep the water backwards. This helps your body turn forwards and then over.

▲ STEP 4
From here, continue sweeping, but unbend your legs to get them down on to the pool floor.

Snorkelling

If you like swimming underwater you may want to consider joining a swimming club that features snorkelling.

Snorkelling uses a large mask, fins and an air tube called a snorkel to allow you to cruise along with ease looking down at the pool floor or seabed.

And if snorkelling tempts you, think about sub-aqua when you get older. Sub-aqua features an air tank strapped to your back which allows you to swim deeper underwater and for much longer periods. Sub-aqua diving clubs provide careful instruction. Contact your local swimming pool for further details.

10 Dive! Dive! Dive!

The big advantage of diving into the water rather than just jumping in is that it puts you straight away into a swimming position. It's vital if you want to swim competitively. Even if you don't, it looks pretty cool. But only if it's done right.

THERE'S ALWAYS A FIRST TIME

There's lots of good technique and skill in diving well, but that's not the problem for most swimmers who can't dive. Their problem is the 'f' word – FEAR.

First of all, don't worry if you're a bit nervous. You see, your mind is thinking, no, this isn't a good idea and it overrules your body. In everyday life, this is a good thing, but in diving you've got to let your body do the talking. You can build up to your first dive as slowly as you want. There are plenty of top competition divers and swimmers who found it hard to dive at first.

Building confidence

You can build your confidence in a number of ways. You must be comfortable about water hitting your face, so practise jumping into the water. Diving while already in the water is a good confidence and technique builder. See the section on underwater swimming (pages 72-77) for more on this.

YOUR FIRST DIVE

Some people are scared of diving because when they're standing on the edge of the pool, it seems a long drop to the water. The solution is to reduce the height between the pool and your eyes. There are two practice dives that do this – the sitting and kneeling dives.

Diving while already in the water – called a surface dive – is a good confidence and technique builder. (See also page 73.)

Diving checklist

1 Only think about learning to dive once you can swim well in water out of your depth. You need 1.8m of water to learn to dive in, at the very least.
2 Only dive in controlled surroundings, such as a pool with a smooth, flat bottom.
3 Have an experienced teacher with you at all times.
4 Never wear goggles when learning to dive.

Sitting dive

The sitting dive is a very valuable part of diving training.

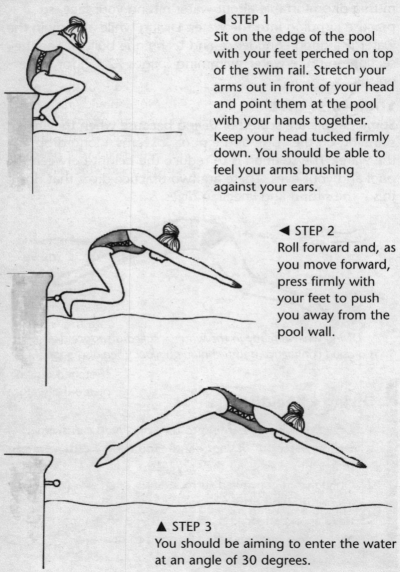

◀ STEP 1
Sit on the edge of the pool with your feet perched on top of the swim rail. Stretch your arms out in front of your head and point them at the pool with your hands together. Keep your head tucked firmly down. You should be able to feel your arms brushing against your ears.

◀ STEP 2
Roll forward and, as you move forward, press firmly with your feet to push you away from the pool wall.

▲ STEP 3
You should be aiming to enter the water at an angle of 30 degrees.

Kneeling dive

This is ideal for a deck-level pool or as a stage up from the sitting dive.

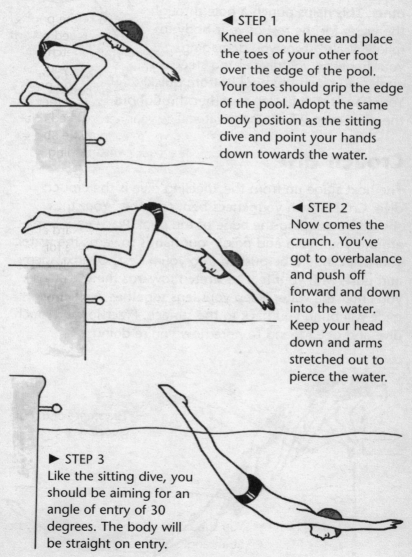

◀ STEP 1
Kneel on one knee and place the toes of your other foot over the edge of the pool. Your toes should grip the edge of the pool. Adopt the same body position as the sitting dive and point your hands down towards the water.

◀ STEP 2
Now comes the crunch. You've got to overbalance and push off forward and down into the water. Keep your head down and arms stretched out to pierce the water.

▶ STEP 3
Like the sitting dive, you should be aiming for an angle of entry of 30 degrees. The body will be straight on entry.

More pool-side dives

With all the dives shown here, hold
your hands together, one over the
other. This helps punch a hole through
the water for the rest of your body to
follow. It also stops you damaging
your fingers if you dive at too steep an
angle and reach the pool bottom quickly.
Your hands should stay together throughout
the dive, even when underwater.

*Good hand
position*

Crouch dive

The next stage up from the kneeling dive is the crouch
dive. Crouch with your knees bent together. Your toes
should be gripping the edge of the pool. Place your arms
around your head and point your hands towards the water.
Your chin should be pushed into your chest. Overbalance
and push with your feet to stretch towards the water. As
you enter the water, keep your legs together. A shallow
glide will bring you back to the surface. Practise the crouch
dive and get a friend to note how you're doing.

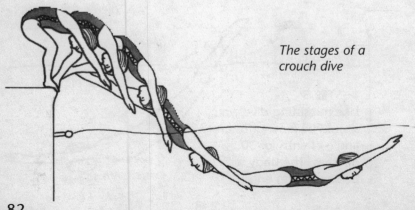

*The stages of a
crouch dive*

The plain header dive

This is a more advanced dive that can be learned from the pool-side and eventually tried out on a springboard. (You'll want a coach to help you.) Attempt a plain header dive in a proper diving pit or in at least 3m of water.

Good Y-shaped starting position

Spring up and over the water

Hips rise and legs straighten

Arms and legs straight

A good entry will be nearly vertical

Diving fault finder

If your dives aren't all that you want them to be, check these tips.

KEEPING IT TOGETHER

When in the standing position, keep your tum and behind tucked in. Your toes must be over the edge. Keep your upper body taut and your legs together as much as possible throughout the dive.

Bad diving stance

STOP THE FLOP!

Bellyflops are when your body hits the water almost flat on. They are usually accompanied by an enormous splash and sniggers from other divers. Bellyflops from the side of the pool are sometimes painful, they can sting a little and they're definitely uncool.

How are they caused? By not getting your hips up high enough and not keeping your head tucked in. Concentrate on forcing your head down into your chest as you dive. It must stay there throughout the dive.

Head not tucked in

Arms and legs apart

Over the arm

A common problem is not getting your hips up high enough. Here's a fun exercise to help you practise springing and bending from the hips.

▲ **STEP 1**
Get a friend to stand in the water with one arm below the water's surface. From a standing position, dive over their arm. See how much you have to bend your body to clear their arm without your body or legs touching it.

▲ **STEP 2**
Coaches reckon your body must bend about 130 degrees to get a good diving angle. As you improve, get your friend to gradually raise the height of their arm until it is on the surface of the water.

Diving for points

Competition diving uses the highboard and springboard. Divers usually have to perform compulsory set dives and some that they can choose themselves. A panel of judges awards marks to each dive. This mark is multiplied by the degree of difficulty – a figure given to each type of dive depending on whether it's hard or easy.

Highboard and competition diving

You'll need specialist coaching to use the high boards in
diving and to enter competitions. Competition divers train
hard. Here's an example of a competition dive.

INWARD DIVE, PIKED

Starting position for this dive is backwards. Diver springs up
and away from the board. The time a diver is in the air is
called the flight.

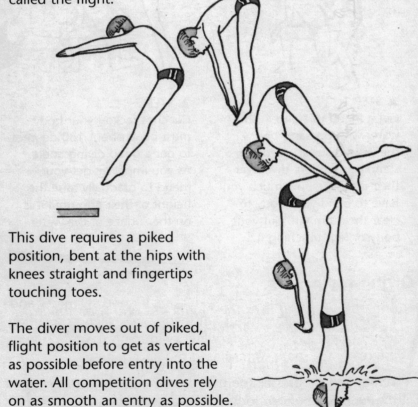

This dive requires a piked
position, bent at the hips with
knees straight and fingertips
touching toes.

The diver moves out of piked,
flight position to get as vertical
as possible before entry into the
water. All competition dives rely
on as smooth an entry as possible.
A big splash means lost points.

11 | Water games

If you are confident in the water, are a good swimmer and have mastered the important techniques, such as treading water (page 21) and underwater swimming (page 72), you are ready for some water-based fun and games.

Whether it's a proper sport like water polo or just a game of tag, you will be able to have brilliant fun with your friends. Water games are also a great way to get fit!

Water polo

This game is a tough, competitive sport which has been part of the Olympics since 1900. There's plenty of rough and tumble, but the water helps cushion bumps and bangs.

It's a seven-a-side game with four substitutes on the bench. The aim is simply to get the ball into the three-metre wide goal. Teams pass and shoot using powerful throws. You are allowed to tackle opposing players. Competition water polo is played in a pool a minimum of one metre deep (in the Olympics, it's 1.8m deep). The pool is between 20 to 30m long and eight to 20m wide. Goals are at least 0.9m above the surface of the water.

HOW THE PROS DO IT

One team wears blue swimming caps, the other wears white. Goalkeepers wear red caps. There are referees and goal judges. Referees decide on foul tackles, such as holding or hitting an opponent. The referees also decide which team the ball should go to if it leaves the pool or bounces off the side.

The game starts with both teams behind their goal line. The referee drops the ball into the middle of the pool and the players swim furiously to get possession. The game is split into four seven-minute quarters of play. The clock is stopped when there's a break in play. It may not sound like a long time, but with players not allowed to touch the bottom of the pool and with super-fast swimming, passing and tackling, it's quite long enough, thank you!

To play water polo, you need to be fit, have good stamina and be an excellent swimmer. If that sounds like you (and 13 of your friends) then here's some advice:

1 Ask for permission to take over the pool. It is unlikely that you will be allowed to play in a public pool during regular swimming sessions.

2 Make goals by stacking kickboards at either end of the pool. The goal mouth should be about 2m or so wide.

3 Don't manhandle opposition players, but you can block their shots and passes.

Ready to play? Right, here are a few handy skill tips.

SURFACE GRAB

▶ If the ball's on the surface, push it down a little into the water. As it bobs up, get your hand underneath the ball and scoop it up.

CATCHING THE BALL

◀ As the ball comes towards your hand, move your hand and arm back to cushion it as you catch it. This technique leaves your hand and the ball in the starting position for a basic throw, which means you can pass or shoot quickly.

THROWING MOVE

▶ Get your arm back behind your head and keep it almost straight to make a throw. Kick your legs so that you rise out of the water and your throw will clear your opponents. You can also make a short push pass as shown right.

Water volleyball

Great fun! Water volleyball is very similar to volleyball on land. Two equally-numbered teams (ideally between three and seven-a-side), try to keep a ball up without it touching the surface of the water. The water cushions falls and really allows you to go for your diving saves and blocks.

Each team is allowed three touches before the ball must pass to the opponent's side. If you're having difficulty, you can increase the number of touches.

Ideally, you need an equal depth of water and a net going across the middle of the pool. If that's not possible, mark out a 'net' with floats on the pool edge. A parents versus children game is made fairer by giving the adults the deep end of a sloping pool.

Water basketball

You need a special pool basketball hoop for this.

Played a lot like water polo, you pass the ball between your team-mates trying to achieve a good shooting position to get the ball through the hoop. Obviously, dribbling isn't too successful so the game becomes a lot more like netball. Swimming in short, fast bursts and changing direction helps get you free of opposition players.

Swimming games

Water polo, basketball and volleyball all involve swimming skills, but the main point of each game isn't actual swimming. The following pages show some games in which swimming is the most important part.

WATER RELAYS

Water relays are fun races between teams of swimmers. Swimmers swim lengths or widths of the pool and tag the next member of their team when they've completed their swim. The winning team is the first to complete the final lap. Have different relay races using different strokes. A team that loses at front crawl may win at breaststroke, back crawl or butterfly.

UNDERWATER RELAY

This game uses a baton. Choose something that you can hold in your hand easily but is heavy enough not to float. Teams line up at one end of the relay course. The batons are placed halfway along the course on the pool bottom. Each swimmer must swim to the baton, retrieve it, and swim to the far end of the course before replacing it in the middle of the pool as they return to their team.

HUNT THE TREASURE

The treasure can be coins or small weights placed in the middle of the pool with the swimmers arranged evenly around the sides. There's one less coin than swimmers. On the referee's whistle, the swimmers dive down and recover a coin. Anyone who shoves is shown the red card!

The swimmer who doesn't find treasure, drops out, and a coin is removed. The winner is the one swimmer remaining at the end.

STATUES

This is a game of tag with a catcher and other swimmers. When a player is tagged, he or she must stand still like a statue with their legs apart. If another swimmer manages

to swim through their legs, they can move again. When all swimmers are statues, the longest-standing statue becomes the catcher.

Play this game in a relatively small area to give the catcher a chance.

WOLF AND LAMBS

A game of 'it' or 'tag' played in water below head height. It starts off with one wolf swimming around trying to touch or tag other swimmers, the lambs. When a swimmer is tagged, they too become a wolf. The winner is the last remaining lamb. In a large pool, it can make for a more interesting game if there are two wolves at the start.

UNDERWATER HOCKEY

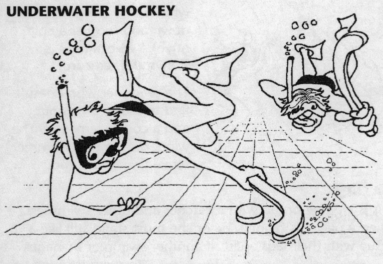

If you thought water basketball was strange, check out this crazy sport. Underwater hockey, or Octopush as it's sometimes called, is played by a growing band of nutty swimmers. A puck is weighted to stay on the bottom of the pool and the aim is to hit it with a stick into the opposing team's goal.

Much of the game actually takes place on the surface as players recover their breath and sprint around the pool before diving down to compete. No contact with other players is allowed and the game is surprisingly fast. Good breath-holding and excellent swimming skills are needed.

All together now

Synchronised swimming was the brunt of lots of jokes
when it first appeared, but people have now started
to take it seriously – especially after trying it. Good
synchronised swimming requires loads of strength,
concentration and swimming skills. What exactly is it?
Well, it's an organised pattern of dance and movement
sequences performed to music. Some people call it water
ballet. But with twists, somersaults and strength holds, it's
more like water gymnastics.

Synchronised swimmers perform routines lasting up to five
minutes and consisting of a number of individual moves, all
set to music. There are events for solo swimmers, duets and
groups of between four and eight swimmers. The music is
played underwater so the swimmers can hear it!

Water games

Solo synchronised swimmers must move in time with the music. Swimmers in groups have double the task, trying to keep in time with both the music and the other members of their team.

Competition synchronised swimmers wear matching swimsuits and tend to use nose clips to aid their breathing.

LEARN THE MOVES

There are hundreds of moves in synchronised swimming. Some, like the difficult dolphin and the Eiffel Tower, have become quite famous.

Most moves begin with certain basic starting positions, often known as layouts. These are then developed into other moves. Apart from great strength, synchronised swimmers use lots of sculling to stay stable in the water and to change position.

Group synchronised swimmers can perform some amazing moves and patterns. And did you realise that when they form those static human pyramids, not one swimmer has their feet on the floor of the pool. Pretty amazing!

Synchronised judging

In competition, panels of at least three judges award points based on smoothness and accuracy. Both the individual moves and the overall routine are given marks. The score is usually out of 10 with one point automatically deducted if any swimmer touches the floor of the pool.

Olympic sport

Synchronised swimming was first admitted to the Olympics as a sport in 1984, but it has been around for a lot longer than that. The United States has had national competitions since 1945 and it was included in the World Swimming Championships for the first time in 1973.

TWO COMMON MOVES

▶ LEGS UP!
Draw both legs towards your chest and then stick them straight up into the air. If you find this hard to do, try it with just one leg, keeping the other leg flat on the water.

◀ INVERTED VERTICAL
This is a tough move to perform. Your body is underwater, one leg is parallel to the water and the other is sticking vertically out of the water. The hands and arms scull constantly to hold the position.

GO THE FLAMINGO!

The Flamingo is an often-used synchronised swimming move that you can try out for yourself. This sequence shows a graceful way of getting to the Flamingo position.

▶ STEP 1
Start by
floating on
your back.

▶ STEP 2
Bend one leg and draw
the foot up
to your
bottom. Keep the
body flat in the water.

▶ STEP 3
Straighten the bent leg and
point it gracefully into the air.
This is called the ballet leg
position.

▶ STEP 4
Draw the knee of the
other leg toward your
chest. Your
hips will sink
below the water. This is
the Flamingo position.

12 Swimming to win

Swimming is a naturally competitive sport. Some who get hooked can't wait to test themselves in competition. But for other swimmers, racing and swim meets hold no appeal. It doesn't matter which type of swimmer you are so long as you always enjoy your swimming. That's the most important thing.

If you feel the urge to compete, you can, no matter how fast or slow you are, what stroke you prefer or even how advanced your technique. Somewhere, some time, there will be a swimming competition to suit you: at your local pool, in a club or even representing your school or town.

Swimming to win

Don't expect to get picked for the Olympics just yet! If you've got a natural talent and are dedicated enough to train very hard, then you could go far.

SETTING YOURSELF TARGETS

Before you compete with others, compete against yourself. Set your own personal targets and really push to match and then beat them. Increase both the overall distance you can swim with the different strokes as well as speeding up your time for each stroke.

TYPES OF SWIMMING RACES

Races can be any distance from 25m to 1500m. Turning at the pool ends and changing direction slows a swimmer down which is why short course records in a 25m pool are slower than long course ones in a 50m pool.

Each of the four major strokes has races of different distances. Freestyle allows you to pick your stroke. In practice, all freestyle swimmers use front crawl because it's the fastest stroke. The world record for 50m is under 22 seconds for men and 24.5 seconds for women. Now that's fast!

The Paralympics

Top swimmers dream of winning of a gold medal in the Olympics, or if they have a disability, the Paralympics. The Paralympics feature various swimming races for competitors grouped according to the level of their disability. The winning swimmers are top athletes in their own right and train just as hard as swimmers in the regular Olympics.

Racing skills

There are whole books written on competition swimming skills. Here is just some basic information on the major moves. Once you've got these starts and turns under control, a swimming coach can help you refine them.

ON YOUR BLOCKS, GET SET ...

▶ A good start is vital in swimming races. Butterfly, freestyle and breaststroke can all use the racing plunge (see page 103) for a clean, fast start. Brush up on your basic diving before trying out this starting position.

A BIG FINISH

▼ Timing, timing, timing – these are the three big secrets of finishing. You, and only you, can make the big decision – whether to start a new stroke or to lengthen your last one and really reach out for the wall. A mistimed lunge that leaves you short of the pool wall can lose you the race or a place. Experience counts for a lot in finishing and top swimmers practise their finishes under the eye of their coaches. As you approach the finish, kick hard and stretch to reach the wall.

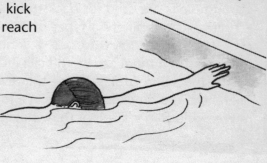

In breaststroke and butterfly races, you must touch the wall with both hands. In all other strokes, one hand is enough.

THE OLYMPIC POOL AND COMPETITIONS

• An official pool is at least 1.8m deep and is 50m long. A short course pool is 25m in length.

• Straight line marking down each lane ends in a T shape. When making forward tumble turns, this T is used as a marker by swimmers.

• Flags across the pool give backstroke swimmers a marker for when the pool wall is approaching.

• The best competition pools are deck level pools where the water is level with the edge of the pool.

• Swimming lanes are usually 2.5m wide. They are separated by rows of special plastic discs that help cut down the waves from swimmers in neighbouring lanes. They're called anti-turbulence lines.

• A false start rope is held 15m down the course. If a false start occurs, the rope is dropped into the water to stop the race.

• Pacing clocks, usually mounted on the wall at the end of the pool, have a giant second-hand. They're used by coaches and swimmers in training.

• Electronic timers are accurate to 1/1000th of a second although most race rules only time to the nearest 1/100th of a second.

• Starting blocks give swimmers a better start.

• Handles mounted onto the pool wall below each starting block are used for backstroke starts.

• There are four different types of official at a swimming race. The starter's job is to, yes, you guessed it – start the race. Then there are the official judges who check on the turns and strokes to see that everything is fair. There is also a timekeeper to record the times and a referee who is in charge of the whole competition.

Racing plunge

The racing plunge is a shallow dive. The key to a successful one is a starting position that coils you up like a spring ready to fly forwards.

On the start signal, pull up with your hands. Your body should overbalance. As your knees bend more, swing your arms forward and bring your head up to see where you're aiming for. Push off with your legs and bend your body. Get your head between your arms with your hands tucked closely together.

Unlike basic dives, you don't want to just fall forward. Look to spring away from the side as fast and hard as you can. Hold the glide until you start to slow then kick hard and make your first arm stroke. This will bring you to the surface of the water.

Try to raise your hips and bottom when in the dive. This helps pull your legs up so your body follows your arms through the hole they have made in the water.

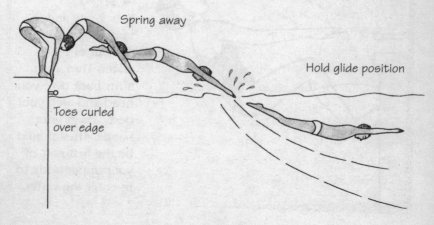

Spring away

Hold glide position

Toes curled over edge

Back crawl racing start

Your toes must stay in the water during the start. Keep your feet together and point your toes. You want them as close to the surface of the water as possible, but still in the water.

STEP 1
▶ When the starter calls "take your marks", coil up like you would in a basic start, only tighter. When the race starts, pull your weight up with your arms and push as hard as you can with your feet away from the wall.

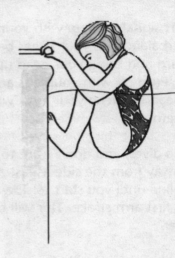

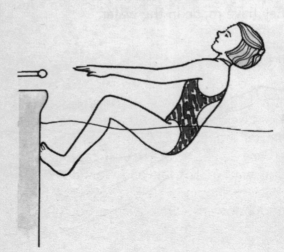

◀ STEP 2
Your body and upper legs should rise out of the water. Throw your arms back over your head and arch your body. Point your hands. They should be the first part of your upper body to re-enter the water.

▲ STEP 3

Keep your hands stretched as you glide through the water. You will soon get used to recognising the moment when your glide starts to lose speed. That is the point when you start swimming the back crawl. Some swimmers prefer to do two or three dolphin kicks before starting the proper back crawl leg kick.

▲ STEP 4

Get a strong kicking action going first before bringing your arms into the stroke.

GET OFF TO A SPEEDY START

1 Don't stick your arms up in the air. In the back crawl start it's important that you get your arms round and behind your head before you re-enter the water.

2 The whole point of the racing start is to get clear of the water to gain speed. Practise pushing off with your feet as hard as possible and work on arching your back as shown in step 3. Together, the arched back and a powerful drive will get you off to a great start.

Turn and burn!

Apart from single-length sprints, all races involve you turning at the pool end. There are rules for how you turn for each stroke.

A good way to practise the turns is to swim widths rather than lengths. Whether you swim lengths or widths, make sure you are clear of people when attempting any turns.

Throwaway turn

Without realising it, you probably already perform a rough throwaway turn when you swim lengths using one of the front strokes. It's the simplest turn and also the slowest. We may be able to speed you up a bit, though, with these tips.

As your leading hand touches the pool wall, bend your arm and turn your body on its side. Tuck your knees up and bring your head up. This allows you to swing your feet round so they touch the pool wall. Push off first with your hand and then strongly with your feet. Try to glide away from the wall in a streamlined shape.

Breaststroke and butterfly turn

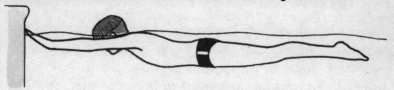

▲ STEP 1
Touch the pool wall with both hands at the same time. As you touch, bend your arms and twist your body up and to one side. Your head should get quite close to the pool wall.

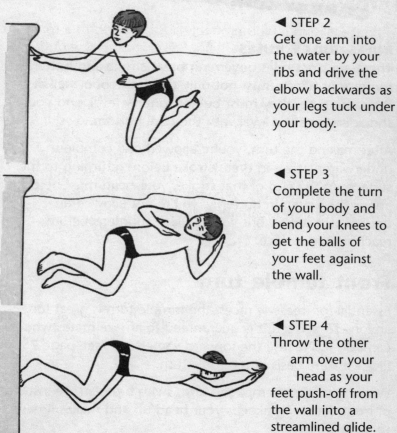

◀ STEP 2
Get one arm into the water by your ribs and drive the elbow backwards as your legs tuck under your body.

◀ STEP 3
Complete the turn of your body and bend your knees to get the balls of your feet against the wall.

◀ STEP 4
Throw the other arm over your head as your feet push-off from the wall into a streamlined glide.

Top tip

Try not to slow down too much when approaching the pool wall. Apart from slowing you down overall, you will need some of your speed to make the turn. If you stretch out and are just short of the pool wall, don't swim an extra stroke. Instead, kick hard to bring you up to the wall. Practice will soon have you judging the distance well.

RULES, RULES, RULES

There are strict rules governing breaststroke and butterfly turns. Your hands must not only touch the pool wall at the same time, they must be horizontally level, and your shoulders must be level with the pool bottom.

After making the turn, you're allowed one complete underwater stroke in breaststroke before returning to the surface. At the end of that stroke, your head must be back above the water. In butterfly, you're not allowed an underwater stroke, but you can kick your legs before reaching the surface.

Front tumble turn

Essential for freestyle races, the tumble turn is great for anyone to perfect. It is guaranteed to amaze mates who can't do it. Practise the forward somersault (see page 75) first – it's the basis of a tumble turn.

When you first attempt the turn, swim breaststroke instead of front crawl. This keeps your head up and makes it easier to tumble forward.

108

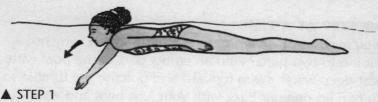

▲ STEP 1

Keep your speed up and don't take a breath on your last stroke.
As you approach the pool wall, duck your head down firmly.

◀ STEP 2
Dolphin kick
your legs
down hard.
Keep your
head down
and get your
knees bent
so your feet
come close to
the pool wall.

◀ STEP 3
Plant your
feet on the
pool wall and
push off. As
you push off,
you should be
turning to
your side.

▲ STEP 4
Drop one shoulder to help your body twist to the side and
then on to your front as you move away. Start the arm
stroke to bring your body to the surface.

109

ONE STEP AT A TIME

If you're struggling with the front tumble turn, why not split it into two parts? Find an empty part of the pool with chest-deep water, swim forward and practise the tumble so you end up on your back with your legs bent and your arms above your head.

Now practise just the push off and twist from the pool wall. Drop down under the water on your back with your knees bent. Push off from the wall and twist around on to your front. Aim to end up on your front with your arms stretched out ahead of you.

Back tumble turn

This is the turn you use when swimming the back crawl. Beware old-fashioned swimming books. The rules have recently changed and you can now turn on to your front and touch the end with your feet instead of your hands.

This makes your turn a lot simpler than before. Still, don't be surprised if you don't get it right first, second or even third time!

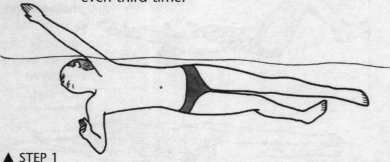

▲ STEP 1

Make your last arm stroke when you're about two body lengths short of the wall. As your arm reaches the vertical, bring it over and across your body. Your other arm pulls through the water to your side. These arm movements help you roll on to your front.

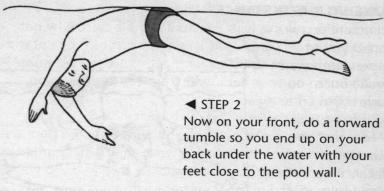

◄ STEP 2
Now on your front, do a forward
tumble so you end up on your
back under the water with your
feet close to the pool wall.

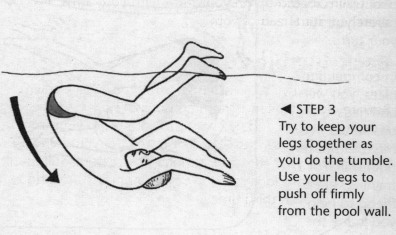

◄ STEP 3
Try to keep your
legs together as
you do the tumble.
Use your legs to
push off firmly
from the pool wall.

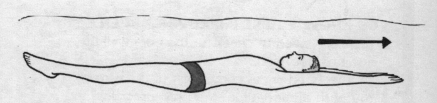

▲ STEP 4
Keep a streamlined position and as the speed of your glide
starts to fade, kick your legs to bring you to the surface.

JUDGING THE DISTANCE

Competition rules forbid you to make another arm stroke once you have rolled on to your front. This means that you have to get the distance from the pool wall correct before you start your turn.

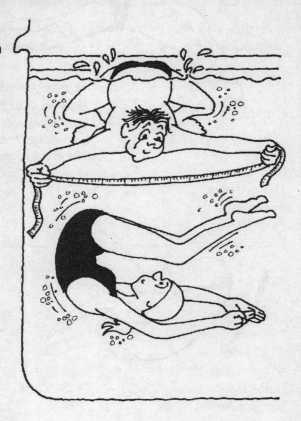

In competition races, you will find flags positioned five metres from the pool wall. For training, get a friend to help you judge the right distance.

YOU KNOW YOU'RE IMPROVING WHEN...
1 You don't need to check for the pool wall by turning your head.
2 Your feet and knees come clear of the water.
3 You push off and glide smoothly just below the surface of the water.

112

What's a medley race?

A medley is a race where swimmers have to use all four main strokes.

Team medley races are relays featuring four swimmers, each swimming one type of stroke. The order is backstroke, breaststroke, butterfly and freestyle. Individual medleys involve one swimmer swimming all four strokes in a different order: butterfly, backstroke, breaststroke and freestyle.

NOT AT THE SAME TIME, PETER!

A medley race is a tough test of your swimming skills. Even the best swimmers have a weakest stroke. The secret is to work hard on this stroke to try to bring it up to the level of your others. A coach will help you on the transition turns that you need to make between each different stroke.

Where do you go from here?

If you're really into swimming, you can join a club, get advice from an experienced swimming coach and aim for the top! Having won a swimming-based competition, I know what a great feeling it is.

Okay, so all I got was a first prize certificate for winning a poolside knobbly knees contest, but everyone has to start somewhere.

You don't have to join a club to improve your swimming. Set yourself some reasonable targets for swimming distance, speed and diving. For example : "By next term, I will move from a sitting dive to a proper, crouch dive." There are even organisations (listed on pages 117-119) who can help you set targets and award you badges and medals when you achieve them.

Want to know more?

If you want want some more reading for those few moments when you are out of the water, try these:

Usborne Hotshots: Swimming
Usborne Publishing

The Handbook of Swimming
David Wilkie and Kelvin Juba
Pelham Books

Swimming
J Verrier
The Crowood Press

The Young Swimmer
J. Rouse
Dorling Kindersley

Learn to Swim In A Weekend
Sharron Davies
Dorling Kindersley

The Essential Swimmer
Steve Tarpinian
Lyons & Burford
For the serious, competitive swimmer, this book has lots of training and technique tips.

Know The Game: Diving
A & C Black
Plenty of step-by-step pictures and helpful instructions.

Join a club

If you're improving your swimming
but want to learn more, think
about joining a swimming club.
Most town swimming pools play
host to one or more swimming
clubs. There, you can get expert
tuition to improve your
swimming technique as well as
meet other swimmers. You can
take part in training exercises
and test your swimming skills
by taking awards.

There are many different swimming
awards (there is some information about
these on the next page) and skill tests including certificates
for distance and speed swimming, water polo, synchronised
swimming, lifesaving and diving.

The way to tap into your nearest
swimming club is to simply contact your
local swimming pool and find out
when the club meets. The rules of
joining will vary from club to club,
so it's best to go along to a club
session and speak to the
membership secretary.

Sign on with an association

There are lots of associations that champion the swimmer and can provide further details on any aspect of swimming.

UNITED KINGDOM AND REPUBLIC OF IRELAND
The Amateur Swimming Association (ASA)
This is the national organisation responsible for swimming and most water sports in Britain. It runs awards schemes and publishes a regular magazine called *Swimming Times*.

Contact the ASA at Harold Fern House, Derby Square, Loughborough, Leicestershire, LE11 0AL.
Tel: 01509 618700.

For details of the ASA awards schemes, write to ASA Awards Centre, 1 Kingfisher Enterprise Park, 50 Arthur Street, Redditch, Worcs, B98 8LG, or phone 01527 514288.

Welsh Amateur Swimming Association (WASA)
Roath Park House, Ninian Road, Cardiff, CF2 5ER
Tel: 029 204 8820

WASA follows the ASA awards schemes.

The Scottish Amateur Swimming Association (SASA)
Holm Hills Farm, Greenlees Road, Camburslang, Glasgow, G72 8DT
Tel: 0141 641 8818

For details of the SASA awards schemes, write to The Scottish Swimming Awards, 44 Frederick Street, Edinburgh, EH2 1EX, or phone 0131 225 7271 between 10am-2pm.

Want to know more?

The Irish Amateur Swimming Association (IASA)
The House of Sport, Long Mile Road, Dublin 12, Ireland.
Tel: (00 353) 1 456 8698

IASA is only open to the public on certain days of the
week, so phone before visiting or better still, contact
them in writing.

Royal Lifesaving Society (United Kingdom)
Mountbatten House, Studley, Warwickshire, B80 7NN
Tel: 01527 853943

Swimming Teachers' Association (STA)
This is a charity that helps teach swimming, lifesaving and
survival techniques. The STA has more than 50 different
award programmes.

Contact the STA at Anchor House, Birch Street, Walsall,
West Midlands, WS2 8HZ.
Tel: 01922 645097, e-mail: sta@sta.co.uk

WORLD SWIMMING RULING BODY
Fédération Internationale de Natation Amateur (FINA)
This is the international organisation responsible for all
competitive racing. Its website comes complete with all the
latest world swimming records.

Contact FINA at Avenue de Beaumont 9, 1012 Lausanne,
Switzerland, or on their website: http://www.fina.org/

AUSTRALIA
Australian Amateur Swimming Association (AASA)
Suite 21a, 56 Nerida Street, Chatswood, NSW 2067.

Royal Lifesaving Society (Australia)
PO Box 321, St Leonards, NSW 2065.

Australian Swimming Inc
Po Box, 169 Kippax, ACT 2615.

Swimming In Australia is a website for competitive
swimmers but it also has lots of great links to other
Australian swimming sites.
http://www.netspace.net.au/~logan/links.html

NEW ZEALAND
New Zealand Amateur Swimming Association
PO Box 11-115, Wellington.

INTERNATIONAL
http://www.swimnews
As its name suggests, Swimnews
carries all the latest news
from around the world regarding
swimmers and swimming.

Glossary

Bilateral breathing – when you take a breath in from one side, then from the other side.

Bow wave – a wall of water in front of your head created when you swim fast.

Catch – the point when your hand starts to create pressure on the water as you start your arm stroke.

Cycle – one set of arm or leg movements.

Exhalation – breathing out.

Extension – straightening a joint such as the elbow through a swimming movement.

Flex – another word for bend.

Fly – increasingly used, cool word for butterfly.

Inhalation – breathing in.

Limb track – the path taken by an arm or leg through a swimming stroke.

Meet – short for a swim meeting or competition.

Piking – bending the hips but not the knees.

Prone – your position when you are face-down in the water.

Recovery – the part of your stroke where your arm doesn't exert any force on the water. It usually means the part of the stroke that gets your arm or leg back to the start of its stroke.

Resistance – how water acts against your body and slows you down.

Stroke cycle – one complete arm and leg action of a stroke.

Supine – your position when you are on your back, face upwards.

Swim off – like a play off in soccer, it's often a race between two or three swimmers to determine who enters the final when dead heats and identical times have created too many swimmers for a final.

Trickle breathing – breathing gently out through the nose and mouth between breaths in.

Index

Index

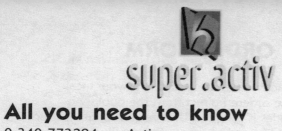

super.activ

All you need to know

0 340 773294	Acting	£3.99	☐
0 340 764686	Athletics	£3.99	☐
0 340 791578	Basketball	£3.99	☐
0 340 791535	Cartooning	£3.99	☐
0 340 791624	Chess	£3.99	☐
0 340 791586	Computers Unlimited	£3.99	☐
0 340 79156X	Cricket	£3.99	☐
0 340 791594	Drawing	£3.99	☐
0 340 791632	Film-making	£3.99	☐
0 340 791675	Fishing	£3.99	☐
0 340 791519	Football	£3.99	☐
0 340 76466X	Golf	£3.99	☐
0 340 778970	Gymnastics	£3.99	☐
0 340 791527	In-line Skating	£3.99	☐
0 340 749504	Karate	£3.99	☐
0 340 791640	The Internet	£3.99	☐
0 340 791683	Memory Workout	£3.99	☐
0 340 736283	Pop Music	£3.99	☐
0 340 791551	Riding	£3.99	☐
0 340 791659	Rugby	£3.99	☐
0 340 791608	Skateboarding	£3.99	☐
0 340 791667	Snowboarding	£3.99	☐
0 340 791616	Swimming	£3.99	☐
0 340 764465	Tennis	£3.99	☐
0 340 773332	Writing	£3.99	☐
0 340 791543	Your Own Website	£3.99	☐

Turn the page to find out how to order these books.

ORDER FORM

Books in the super.activ series are available at your local
bookshop, or can be ordered direct from the publisher.
A complete list of titles is given on the previous page. Just tick
the titles you would like and complete the details below.
Prices and availability are subject to change without prior notice.

Please enclose a cheque or postal order made payable to
Bookpoint Ltd, and send to: Hodder Children's Books, Cash Sales
Dept, Bookpoint, 39 Milton Park, Abingdon, Oxon OX14 4TD.
Email address: orders@bookpoint.co.uk.

If you would prefer to pay by credit card, our call centre team
would be delighted to take your order by telephone.
Our direct line is 01235 400414 (lines open 9.00 am – 6.00 pm,
Monday to Saturday; 24-hour message answering service).
Alternatively you can send a fax on 01235 400454.

Title .... First name .... Surname ....

Address ....

....

....

Daytime tel .... Postcode......................................

If you would prefer to post a credit card order, please complete
the following.

Please debit my Visa/Access/Diner's Card/American Express
(delete as applicable) card number:

Signature ....Expiry Date ....

If you would NOT like to receive further
information on our products, please tick ☐ .